# Son of a Sharecropper

# Son of a Sharecropper

Mr. George F. Fitzgerald

To order additional copies of this book, contact:
Xlibris Corporation
1-888-795-4274
www.Xlibris.com
Orders@Xlibris.com
66106

# ACKNOWLEDGMENTS

My knowledge of the Scripture was obtained by attending many church services and listening to thousands of sermons by many Pastors. Being a certified LAY SPEAKER in the local United Methodist Church I feel one of my duties is to realize that God gave me a message to share and I should not keep it to my self.

Mr. George F. Fitzgerald

# CONTENTS

# DEDICATION

In loving memory of my parents, Albert and Mary Ella (Staples) Fitzgerald, my brothers, William H. and Clarence R. Fitzgerald, and my sister, Mary A. Fitzgerald.

In honor of my sister, Grace L. (Fitzgerald) Smith and my brother, James A. Fitzgerald.

Yours truly,
Mr. George F. Fitzgerald

The cover photo shows me as a young man holding my father's favorite gun which he used in his favorite hobby, hunting. He usually went hunting in the fall with a couple of his buddies when he could find the time. That hobby came in handy now and then because it provided additional fresh meat for the dinner table. Notice our tobacco field behind me. My father kept that particular gun above the bedroom door placed in homemade brackets.

Cover designed by Mr. George F. Fitzgerald

My father had older dogs that just lie around and bark if a stranger visited our property, however he also had dogs that hunted foxes and deer, dogs that hunted rabbits, dogs that hunted coons and squirrels and also birds. In other words we had dogs that hunt and point. The fox dogs were a laid back type of dogs when not hunting however when hunting and they pick up the scent of a fox or deer they traveled great distances sometimes arriving back home the next day.

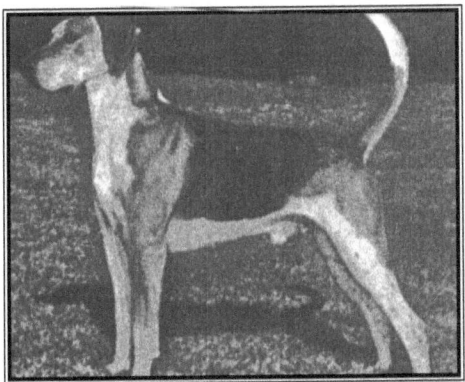

# INTRODUCTION

This book is really a retelling of a segment of Black History because it reveals the history of this Black man's journey on the road to equity. This book is not about a man walking around with a chip on his shoulder or a man who preaches hate. This book is about a Black man forgiving but not forgetting because Gentiles, Jews and various groups of people have made great sacrifices to help me on this long and sometimes difficult journey. Many Black people, including me, have often received the short end of the stick. Although we as a people have made great strides, the journey is not over. The journey is actually continual. As I find myself walking closer to Jesus, I realize I am on the ultimate journey which is the long and righteous journey to salvation, the journey that leads to everlasting life.

—G.F.F.

A SHARECROPPER

A FARMER WHO WORKS ANOTHER'S LAND IN RETURN FOR
A SHARE OF THE CROP OR PROFIT. {usually an unfair share}

I was born on February 23, 1943 in a small town in southwestern Virginia. The same midwife who delivered me had delivered my older sisters and brothers. I was the youngest child in the family. I had three brothers and two sisters; however, one sister and one brother had passed on before I was born. I truly believe that if I trust God and obey His teachings, I will meet them in Heaven one day. I was raised in a five-room house; however, as the years went by, my father added another room on the back to give us a little more space. We had a cooking stove in the kitchen and another stove in the living room which we used for heat. There were many times that I had to cover up under several blankets and quilts to keep warm during those cold winter nights. An icebox was our only source of refrigeration. I remember the iceman coming by once a week delivering ice in 25- and 50-pound blocks. Our water came from a nearby spring, and later on my father had a well dug in our back yard. We kept a jar of water by the well to pour into the pump to prime it and speed up the process of pumping water.

My father was a sharecropper. I did not understand at the time, but I learned later, that he was doing what many Black people were doing then in order to feed their families and earn enough to survive. Although we were poor, we always had food to eat because we planted and grew ninety percent of our food. Because we always had plenty of apples, pears and peaches to go with the vegetables we grew, my mother canned fruit, vegetables, preserves, etc., to carry us over those long winter months. We raised hogs and chickens in order to have fresh meat on the table. My father had little time for hobbies, although he found the time to do a little hunting and fishing, thus adding fresh fish and rabbit, deer and squirrel meat to our menu. Try eating pig's brains and "mountain oysters" (pig's testicles), just to name two parts of a poor man's diet. It took me a few years to discover that a chicken had a breast; however, the pastor of our church knew it because whenever he visited our house for Sunday dinner, he received the best. My father was able to own a car, truck and, eventually, a tractor to help him make a little extra money on the farm.

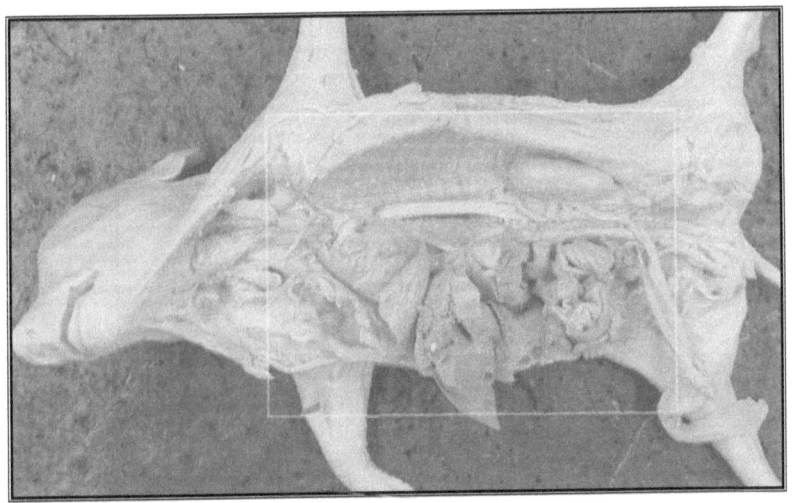

The Interior parts of a hog
We raised and slaughtered hogs for food, not for a sport

I had to walk to school my first couple of years, passing an all-White school on the way. I wondered why I couldn't go to the school that was closer to my home but did not ask any questions. My elementary school was a couple of miles from our house so my father cut down some trees and brush to make a shortcut for my siblings and me. Of course, our school had no cafeteria which meant we had to bring our own lunch. I brought biscuit sandwiches because we had loaf bread on Saturdays and hot rolls on Sundays. Some of the kids whose mothers and fathers could afford to give them loaf bread daily used to laugh at the kids who had biscuits. That was all right; those biscuits served their purpose. The elementary school was a two-room, wood-framed building with a large, wood burning stove in each room. There were some chilly winter days and hot spring days spent in those classrooms yet we survived. Our high school and middle school building was a breath of fresh air. Both schools were in a large brick building which had heat in every room. Although there was no air conditioning, we did not miss what we never had.

In high school, just as in elementary school, we had to learn and behave ourselves because our parents knew our teachers and saw them weekly at the local market or in church. Every day after school, the first thing I had to do was to take off my school clothes and put on the old clothes that my parents called "work clothes." Then I would eat and immediately begin doing chores around the house and on the farm such as chopping wood for the stoves, feeding the chickens, pigs and hogs, milking the cows, and sometimes much more. Most of my work clothes were hand-me-downs. I got used to that practice because most of my books in elementary and high school were used books that we received from the White schools when their books were updated. I learned later on that being poor humbles you, and being poor teaches you to appreciate and take care of what you have; being poor reminds one to thank God daily because it could be worse. To this day, I thank God for His blessing, for I know that it is because of His mercy that I am walking above the ground instead of lying beneath it. Even when I am buried, my soul will ascend to Heaven if I stay on the path of righteousness.

I did not get the opportunity to play high school sports, not only because of the chores after school which all farm boys faced, but also because sports practice times conflicted with the appointed times that the buses left for home. My father worked from sunup until sundown and could not pick me up after practice. I lived several miles from my high school. My high school's teams were very competitive. If memory serves me right, I believe we won several divisional titles as well as state championships. I had opportunities to play in pick-up games on Saturdays where I carried the rock, hit the ball great distances and shot the ball from downtown. Being an athlete was one of the ways to become popular with girls. High school was the time to start paying more attention to girls too. In spite of the fact that southern parents set strict rules about dating, which they sometimes called "courting," they had to realize love was in the air. Although love was filling the air, I had to be very careful not to say too much to White girls; the price for a young Black man was too high in those days. That did not bother me, because I had plenty of beautiful Black girls to choose from in high school.

Our little ten acre farm provided us with most of the food we ate. It also provided opportunities for the rodents to cash in on some of the food. The cats on our farm traveled throughout the barn and around the farm along with snakes to help control the rodent population, provided we did not over feed them. When our cats was a little hungry they spent a geat deal of time creeping and peeping, searching for the rats and mice however if we overfed them, they would just wash their faces, curl up in a ball and sleep most of the day and night.

At times you will notice me moving around in some of my experiences in my life while growing up in the south. I understand I was not alone in those troubled times however I feel I must share them with you and especially the young folks before my mind become fuzzy. Therefore some of my messages will not fall in exact order, they will be told as the events occur to me. My oldest brother William worked at a restaurant in my hometown as a dishwasher back in the early fifties and was responsible for cleaning the dishes, pots, pans, knives, spoons, forks and other items that the white patrons ate out of or ate with but he was not allowed to sat in the very place he worked to eat a snack on his break. When my family worked on the white man's farm sometimes we ate dinner at their house. My mother helped cook and served the food for everyone to eat. We had to eat on the screened in back porch while the white folks ate inside in the dining room. Before they ate they graced their table. I often wondered did they know any better or they just did not care? I often wonder today that if all white folks felt the same way what would been the result of us gaining a little taste of freedom or whether things would remain the same for a longer period of time? There were some whites that did not agree with the way we was treated, however they knew if they went against the system their peers would reject them. Jesus had compassion. The shortest chapter in the bible tells us when Jesus came to the tomb of his friend Lazarus, his respond was immediate, {Jesuswept.} John:11:35 I understand that we cannot change the past, however if we stay on our mission we can continue to change the future. If you give out I can understand, but please do not give up. Young folks, let keep the ball rolling.

Although we were sharecroppers, I was not exposed to a total plantation environment thanks to my grandparents who had purchased the little farm where we lived back in 1903. My father, being the next to youngest child, had decided not to leave home and instead carried on the family tradition. My aunts and uncles had moved up North to Baltimore and New York City to seek greener pastures. We were poor folks, but my parents never thought of going on welfare because that was not part of their mentality. However, if I had the opportunity to make that decision back then, I would have jumped on it right away. Thank goodness that I did not have the need to think about welfare as an adult because I always had a job, in many cases two or three jobs at the same time.

When I was young, we had just one radio station that played Black music in our part of Virginia. Most radio stations in the area played either White artists or White artists trying to sing Black artists' songs. There was a radio station in Tennessee that played all of the best Black music at night. That's how I kept up with the good old soul music on my battery-operated radio. We also had good gospel music at our church on Sundays.

Horses and cows get along together, Why can't we?

Mt. Zion Baptist Church
The church I attended until I relocated to Baltimore Md. in 1961.

Tub similar to the one we used to wash clothes and bathe
in before we progressed to indoor plumbing

As time passed, I understood my father's patience and tolerance and why he had made some of the decisions he made. To keep our family out of harm's way, he preached to us to obey the law no matter how difficult it may seem at the time. He knew that unfair laws would change before long and we would be around to reap the benefits and pass them on to our future families. The White merchants always gave my father credit in their stores because he was a peace-loving man. The merchants usually kept the books and he and the other Black sharecroppers had to rely on the figures they gave them. For a sharecropper, larger sums of money only came at harvest time. The harvest usually began in late August and the season lasted into December, therefore, money was scarce as hen's teeth during the growing season of late spring and early summer.

When high school graduation time rolled around, I was as happy as could be. One reason for my joy was that our parents had encouraged us to finish school, especially my brother James and me, because my oldest brother and sister did not graduate. Another reason was that I considered myself very lucky because the White folks in the county next to the county where I went to school had closed the schools there a year earlier because they did not want to integrate. A third reason was that I had plans to go a little farther North to seek a job where I could make a decent living and get paid weekly or bi-weekly. I understood by then that the very definition of freedom had evolved. Once it had meant simply escaping slavery by going to a state where slavery had been abolished, but now it included achieving equality under the law, increased opportunity and being free from discrimination and violence.

Birds of a feather flock together

Being the youngest child, I was the last to leave home to go out on my own. My two brothers were living in Baltimore and my sister was married and living locally. After I told my father that I was leaving, he tried to persuade me to stay home. He even promised to buy me a car if I stayed and helped him on the farm. I said, "Dad, thanks for the offer, but I feel it will be better for me to go to Baltimore. I will be with my brother and I can seek better job opportunities and a regular paycheck." Then I asked my brother James if he could find anyone in Baltimore that was coming to our hometown in Virginia and he could reserve a ride back to Baltimore for me. I told him that I would graduate on June fifth and be ready to leave on June sixth. My brother got me a ride going up to Baltimore on June seventh. That was good timing. It reminded me of one of my favorite R&B songs, "Good Timing" by Jimmy Jones, which I often played on the jukebox on weekends. For some strange reason, we called a jukebox a "piccolo" in my little town. I would quickly stop doing that after I arrived in Baltimore. I would not need a lot of room during the ride there because I was just a skinny 18-year-old kid traveling with the clothes on my back, everything else I owned stuffed into a cardboard suitcase and a five-dollar bill in my pocket which took me three weeks to save.

After my father realized that he could not change my mind, he said he was going to the store to cash a check so he could give me some money to take with me. However, he was late getting back to me, perhaps in a last-ditch effort to make me change my mind. Before my father left for the store, he told me to do three things. He said, "Son, when you get to Baltimore, do not hang on the corners, get a job. Stay out of trouble." The last thing he said was, "Find a church home." When my ride finally came to pick me up it was noontime. I quickly got into the back seat of that '58 Buick, and since I was just a skinny kid, there was plenty of room for me. As we were ready to drive out of the yard, my mother said, "Make sure to keep in touch." Then she and my sister who was visiting waved with sad looks on their faces and said goodbye.

After riding and talking for about an hour, everyone in the car became quiet. Except for the driver and me, everyone took a nap because that big Buick was such a comfortable ride it made it hard to keep your eyes open. As we traveled northward on Route 301, it finally sunk in that I was actually grown and going out on my own for the first time. Then I started thinking to myself, *No more planting, growing and harvesting crops. No more milking and feeding the cows, and no more feeding chickens, horses and hogs. No more chopping wood, wringing the necks of chickens or slaughtering hogs . . .* There are many good reasons to look back. As scientists learn more about the way the brain processes emotions and stores emotional memory, it will become increasingly clear that yesterday's feelings influence our ability to make and keep emotional connections today.

In 1961 this car was my ride to semi-freedom. At that time I felt I had paid my dues. I was tired of card board in my work shoes and patches on my work clothes I was tired of working all week and at the end of the week I ended up broke. I decided I needed to be in a situation where there was hope. At certain times in a person life he or she has to make choices. With the blessing of God my decision turned out alright. My parents did the best they could at that time and I am still thankful to them. They could not always provided me with all the luxuries I desired however they taught me to be thankful for what I had.

After a couple of stops on our way to Baltimore, I realized that I had not noticed signs separating the races at the restaurants, bathrooms and water fountains. That was a little taste of freedom. After three or four hours, we arrived on Bethel Street in east Baltimore where my cousin lived. My brother James had made arrangements for me to stay with her and her family until we could get our own place. My brother was staying with another family several blocks away. James met me as we arrived and paid the gentleman who brought me to Maryland. I said to myself, *Hello, bright lights!* Once my cousin had introduced me to almost everyone on the block, I went to my room and unpacked my cardboard suitcase. During that time, everyone who was not at work seemed to be sitting on those famous marble front steps watching all the activity that went on in the block.

Where are the trees

I realized that my next mission was to find a job. Of course, I had no transportation, so I had to use the streetcar, bus or walk. Since I developed a fear of getting lost on public transportation, I elected to walk to the different merchants who were within walking distance. I went to bakeries, movie theaters, printing companies and several food markets. After weeks of searching, I landed a job at a food market on Gay Street. The owner hired me after I went there to ask for a job two weeks in a row. He said that he would hire me because I "appeared to really want a job." He hired me and placed me in the meat department. I felt almost at home when I saw the fresh chicken, neck bones, fatback and various kinds of meat. In 1961, the pay rate was low. He gave me fifty cents an hour for forty-seven and a half hours per week to start. I accepted it because I needed a job.

After watching me work the first day, the owner gave me a 25-cent per hour raise. I smiled from ear to ear. They would not let me cut the most expensive meats such as lamb, veal and steak. I was allowed to work with the cheaper cuts like neck bones and fatback, however; my hands were so quick that I did a lot of meat package wrapping. People often stood there and watched me wrap the packages because I was so fast. The market was 10-12 blocks from where I lived. Being a country boy, walking to and from work was no problem. The food market's owner and his wife would pick a few good workers to give a few dollars' worth of groceries to at the end of the week. When I became one of the chosen ones, I would pick ice cream along with canned meats such as Spam and tuna which I used for my lunch during the week. My cousin provided my breakfast and dinner. I was so happy that she charged me very little rent since we were relatives and her husband had grown up near my family in Virginia.

I met my first friend, Richard, at that market. As a matter of fact, we are still friends after over 48 years. After living with my cousin for a couple of years, I decided to get an apartment with my brother James. Since we were both single, sharing an apartment meant we could have whatever guests we desired without worrying about disturbing the families we had been staying with up to that point. Our apartment worked out fine until, a few months later, James was drafted into the military. I remember saying to myself, *My oldest brother William and now James were free to go into the armed forces, but they were not free to go into the voting booth.* When President Johnson signed the Voting Rights Act of 1965, they had both already served or were serving in the military. Since we had been sharing the rent, I needed another job in order to pay the rent and other expenses by myself. As the saying goes, "It made my soul look back and wonder how I got over, dear Lord."

## The Signs Of The Times

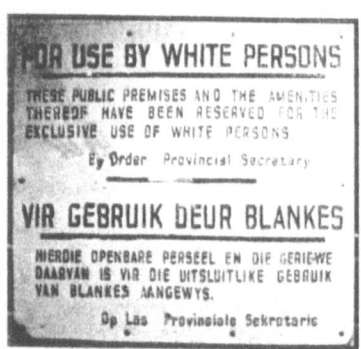

These were some of the signs that I had to deal with during my younger days while growing up in Virginia. As I travel to other places there were some of the same in and outside of the United States

## RACE

My brother had been working for one of Maryland's largest banks, and while he held a relatively menial position, it paid more than what I was making at the

food market. Before he left to serve in the military, he asked his supervisor to hire me in his place. He hired me and it worked out fine. I worked hard and was promoted to the position of manager of the stock room. I became responsible for supplying all branches with various bank forms such as money orders, certified and cashier's checks, etc. I was bubbling with confidence and started attending the Baltimore chapter of the American Institute of Banking in order to prepare myself for future promotions. I also enrolled at the Maryland Institute College of the Arts in case opportunities arose in the advertising department. Then the bank came along and stuck a pin in my bubble. They hired a White gentleman in my department who quickly started asking dozens of questions about its operations. They told me his job was sharing my position. Common sense and mother wit told me not to be confrontational because that would only hurt my chances for a reference when I applied for another job.

I had met my future wife, Carolyn, earlier in 1965 and we had already made plans to get married. I needed to make money and refused to train another man to be my boss. With the little influence I had, I was able to secure a job for Carolyn at the bank before I moved on to greener pastures. Since things were growing sour there for me, however, I worked at the bank in the daytime, worked at a local supermarket in the evenings, and then did cleaning details at a department store until 1:30 a.m. six nights a week. I already had a car and was saving money for furniture and a new apartment once we got married. Our marriage was quickly approaching. Fortunately, my friend Richard was working at a major supermarket chain at that time helped me obtain a job there as a journeyman meat cutter. For the first time in my life, I was making a decent salary and had benefits which I would be able to share with my new wife.

Carolyn and I planned to be married in the late spring or early summer of 1966, about a year after we had first met. I began to realize that I had to take on a more responsible role in life. I loved Baltimore; however, I did not want to live in a small area where I could not enjoy the freedom of having a sizeable yard where the grass could grow between my toes if I let it. Being raised in the country, I needed a little room to stir. You can take a boy out of the country, but you cannot take the country out of him. We purchased our first home, a three-bedroom rancher, in 1972. We quickly outgrew it, however. By that time we had our one and only child and decided to move to a larger home with four bedrooms, a garage and a bigger back yard. The fact that I was making a good salary as a journeyman meat cutter and my wife worked at a large bank enabled us to move from our first one-bedroom apartment in west Baltimore to our first house and then to a larger home in Baltimore County on Christmas Eve, 1975.

We have enjoyed traveling before our retirement because I believe that the future is not promised to anyone on earth. Now that we are retired, we still travel to different places inside and outside of the U.S.A. On my various jobs I had always enrolled in self-help classes and seminars in order to be prepared in case the chance for a promotion presented itself. My good work ethic, together with having quite a bit of experience working around animals on a farm, enabled me to rise from being a part-time journeyman meat cutter to the meat department manager, a rare position for a Black man in one of the larger food chains in Baltimore in the 1960s. There were times when I thought I was Black twice because I was put down by some of my White co-workers because of the color of my skin as well as by my own people because of their jealousy over my rising to a good position. The jealous ones were showing their "crab-like" mentality, always wanting to bring another crab down to the bottom of the barrel with them instead of being happy that one was rising to the top. My father had told me when I was young, "Only the strong survive." I found it to be true.

Although I am happy about most decisions which I have made in my life, including coming to Maryland, there are some things I miss because I was born and raised in the South. Then again, there are some things I do not miss. I did hustle whenever I could, but I don't miss being low on funds most of the time. I also do not miss the Jim Crow laws and restrictions such as separate schools, water fountains, parking spaces and the signs that read "Colored Take-Out Only" and "Colored Orders Taken Around Back." I am aware of the fact that some of these restrictions existed in other parts of the country; however, as I grew older, I began to realize more about the way the country as a whole felt about Black people. Being very young in the South, there was a strange feeling I had when trying to understand why. Among the things that I miss dearly are my mother, my father, and oldest brother, all of whom have passed on to glory, my mom's home cooking, the fresh fruits and vegetables, fresh meat from the pigs which we raised to be slaughtered every fall and fresh eggs from the nest. I also miss the homemade molasses from the sugar cane which we grew and processed on our farm. We raised most everything we ate which meant there was a lot of hard work under the blazing sun that I surely do not miss. The fact that one began life in a humble surrounding does not mean that you cannot rise above that circumstance. Jesus was born in a stable and now He is seated in Heaven on the right side of the Father. Amen?

During my 33-year career in the food industry, I managed or co-managed some of the largest meat departments in the Baltimore area. As a result, I received many performance awards for a job well done. After my son was grown and out on his own, I decided to retire early and pursue some of my childhood dreams. I had always wanted to write and publish books, doodle with flea markets, open my own antiques shop, take my bowling hobby to a higher level and become an active church member. I was able to accomplish all of these things and am still doing them. I currently serve in several ministries for the Epworth Methodist Chapel, and I am enrolled in the Epworth Chapel School of Christian Life and Learning where I am working toward a master's diploma in Christianity. I often think about the many days my parents worked hard every day for very little pay and still served in church on Sundays singing hymns of victory.

My father worked on our little farm until he became ill and could no longer perform the physical labor. After my mother died in 1987, my youngest niece stayed with my father on our farm, caring for him until he had to be admitted to a nursing home. Although my brother James and I lived a few hundred miles away, we were able to visit him on a regular basis. My sister Grace, who lived a few miles away, as well as my nieces, and his friends and fellow church members all visited him weekly if not daily. My father lived in a nursing home for several years and then, twelve days before his ninety-third birthday, he passed away in the year 2003. In fact, at the time of his death, my father was among the oldest living persons in the county. All the landowners that he had worked for had passed on before him but not one of them had given him a dime in his will despite all the wealth that he helped them accumulate.

Newer machinery was coming in when I was leaving

Although I never witness it, some sources say at times
women had to do some heavy lifting

Truck similar to my father's first truck

What is a farm without Horses

Although it seems very slow now, I enjoyed living through the progressions from carrying water from a spring to drink, cook, and clean with to pumping water from a well in our yard to having running water inside our house, from using kerosene lamps and wind-up clocks to having indoor electricity, from owning an icebox to owning a refrigerator, from washing clothes by hand to using a washing machine, and from having neither telephone nor television to having both. Young people today need to know what we had to tolerate in order to keep the ball rolling, thus making it easier for them. It was not easy then. As a youngster, I had a hard time trying to figure out why there were water fountains and bathrooms with signs saying "Colored" and "White." Even the lunchrooms and churches were separate, though I was taught that there was one God and He loved us all. I remember sitting in the balcony to watch a movie while the White folks sat downstairs in the theater, and watching the movie from the last two rows of the drive-in when I paid the same price to get in as the White patrons. I was afraid to ask about it because one would have been considered a troublemaker if he asked too many questions. I had a little trouble figuring out who I really was in years past. First I was called "Boy," and then it was "Colored," and then "Negro," then "Black," and along the way the "N-word." Now I'm called either "Afro-American" or "African-American."

When I was very young, there was only one Black doctor for us, and then later on we went to either the White or Black doctor in the area. I remember when my father had a medical emergency and my oldest brother had to take him to a hospital about 49 miles from our home because they would not treat him at the local White hospital which was a lot closer. When I was a youngster, I remember that we used many home remedies because we could not afford to go to a doctor unless we thought it was a serious illness. If I had a headache or stomachache or even a cold, my mother would go in the kitchen cabinet and take out a bottle of castor oil which usually did the job. If you take it once, you will not try to get any kind of sickness.

There were times when I got a little out of line in public as a child. My mother and father did not have to holler at me or spank me, however; they gave me a certain look and I quickly calmed down and got in line. Sometimes I wondered what I would have done if it were not for those good old gospel songs and that country preaching. That music and preaching kept me motivated. There were times when I was tired of being broke. My parents did give me a little money from time to time; however, as I grew older, I needed extra money so I put my shoulder to the wheel and earned money the old-fashioned, honest way. My parents did not mind it if I did a little hustling, provided my homework and chores were done. They wanted to know what I was doing and whether it was honest work. To make extra money, I did odd jobs for the White folks in the neighborhood, including raking leaves, washing windows and assorted tasks in and around their houses. They would only hire you if they knew your mother and father and trusted them. I also sold such items as creams, oils, liniments, rubbing ointments, flower and vegetable seeds and even a newspaper that had a small circulation. I learned the value of a dollar at an early age.

My Trusty Suitcase

This is the actual suitcase that I packed all my belonging in June 7th 1961
as I traveled to Baltimore Maryland to seek greener pastures

Can you imagine being a salesman in a rural area without transportation, not even a bike? There were long distances between the houses; therefore, I had to take many shortcuts through woods and cow pastures while keeping an eye on the mean bulls guarding their cows. As I traveled, I collected soda bottles I saw along the way so I could redeem them later for a couple of pennies apiece. I also did a little recycling which was not very popular in my town during that time. I had the time because we did not have a swim club and the only way we could swim was in the shallow water of the river with the snakes and frogs. I had seen bowling on television and wanted to bowl, however, we did not have a bowling alley that Black folks could use. In my life, as in the lives of many people of color, I had to make many adjustments and tolerate many unjust situations in order to move forward and reach my goals.

I was blessed while growing up because my parents never abused me and God allowed both my mother and father to live to a ripe old age and see all of us grown and on our own. Growing up was not all bad, even with that Jim Crow society. My parents did not allow us to swear, drink alcohol, or smoke, and drugs were extremely rare in my little town. I saw many things that bothered me during my youth but I managed to learn to accept the things that I could not change. Many times it was not fun working in that blazing sun, especially when I had to plow the hard ground. Nonetheless, I did not let it get me down. I realized that I had to fight through the tough times even when I felt the need to cry. I told myself, "If I cry, very few would care, and I will be left just drowning in my own tears." I refused to sink into the land of gloom and deep darkness. I realized the poor had hope. Therefore, I tried to fill my mouth with laughter and shouts of joy. If you meet any of my classmates, they will tell you this was true.

Over the years I've listened to different pastors preach about my Lord and Savior and, especially after undertaking Bible study, I now feel very blessed after reading how they treated Jesus after all He has done for us. Please remember that He died so that we may live. Learning to survive was a building block for life which helped me struggle through the difficult civil rights movement. Even now I am still struggling to do my little part in making the rough edges smooth and trying to reach out to young folks and let them know that great tasks lie ahead. Young people, stay strong, for there are no shortcuts or easy ways out. Get a quality education, stay out of trouble and do not give society a reason not to hire you. Be a father or a mother for your kids. Use that old-fashioned mother wit.

Hail Foster High!
We pledge our lasting love to thee!
Our voices raised, we'll ever sing your praise
With open minds, we learn, we know no other
Thy name alone, we proudly cheer and raise!

Luther H Foster High School

During the early fifties and sixties, the gas station workers, who were ninety-nine percent White in my town in Virginia, pumped your gas after you paid. When a Black guy moved North and returned to visit family and friends with out-of-state tags on his car, and especially if he was driving a nice car, the gas station workers would say to him, "That's a mighty fancy car you're driving, whose boy are you?" or "How can you afford that? What kind of work do you do?" Over the years people have asked me if I could point to one incident that shaped my views on race, but I cannot. Seeing in person and on television some of the horrible things that went on during the Civil Rights Movement such as police attacking women, children, and men with police dogs, clubs, and water hoses strong enough to rip bark off of trees, the church bombings, assassinations and much more made me realize that Black people, although behaving peacefully, were walking on a slippery slope. Their lives were always in the balance while just trying to get their piece of the American pie.

When I was twelve, a former neighbor who had grown up in my little town and had relocated to Baltimore, returned for a visit and was driving a beautiful, red and black, two-door, 1955 Chevy hardtop. That car immediately caught my eye and I added it as another item on my list of dreams I hoped to make come true after my high school graduation. After I obtained my first job, I began saving as much as I could towards fulfilling my many childhood dreams.

At the age of nineteen, I went to a driving school to practice my driving skills because driving on a farm was a little different from driving in the city. I passed the driving test and received my license a couple of weeks later. After I had saved a few hundred dollars, I started looking for the car of my dreams. I searched around at many different dealerships; however, I could not find my dream car—a 1955 Chevy, two-door hardtop. Since I was so excited about getting a car, I settled for a two-door, powder blue and white 1956 Chevy with red interior.

man with a plan

When I tried to purchase the car, the dealership informed me that I needed to be at least twenty-one. Otherwise, I needed a co-signer. At the time, I was only twenty. I discussed my problem with Mr. Jones, an older gentleman on my job who lived on Broadway in East Baltimore. I had known him for only six months when he said to me, "You seem like a hard working, respectful young man. Therefore, I will co-sign for you." I thanked him and said to myself, *that old country teaching from my mother and father really paid off.* Mr. Jones took me to the dealership, co-signed for the loan, and followed me home to make sure I was alright as a first-time car owner. Now, that's real love and concern.

My Father did a little lumberjacking for extra money and firewood

Shed used for storage of farm equipment

Although during those times you could leave your car unlocked, the windows down, and only had to be concerned if it rained. The first few months after purchasing my car, I got up various times during the night to look out the window to make sure my car was alright. Also, I noticed that very few city boys my age had their own cars. Along with my great charm, having my own car made me very popular with the young ladies. I never made it a habit to drive around with a car load of guys. I always believed that two is a couple and three is a crowd.

I was very proud the first time I went to visit my family in Virginia driving my very own car. I wanted William, my oldest brother who had relocated back to our hometown, to see it first. I also wanted my family and friends to see that another one of my dreams had come true. As a young teenager, I was just trying to make it a little further North where jobs and other opportunities were more available. Over the past 43 years, not only do I still live with my wife in Maryland, we had the pleasure of vacationing in many places such as North Carolina, South Carolina, Georgia, New Orleans, Florida, West Virginia, Delaware, Pennsylvania, New Jersey, New York, Connecticut, Nevada, California, Washington state, Hawaii, Alaska, Canada, Cancun Mexico, Cayman Islands, Jamaica, Freeport and Nassau, Bahamas, Puerto Rico, and Bermuda and look forward to vacationing at many more places. I don't think that's too bad for a poor country boy. I believe all work and no fun makes George a dull boy.

While growing up in the South, I learned many valuable lessons. I learned that anger is many times justified; however, how we react to it is very important. We must not allow ourselves to dwell in the past, but instead use it as a stepping stone for the future by using lessons learned from past experiences to avoid future mistakes. Please do not allow the lack of an education dim your potential bright career nor allow poverty to silence your future. When all is said and done, we must not allow our lure for lust and devilish lifestyles take away our chances for the greatest gift that we can ever receive—ETERNAL LIFE.

I was able to fulfill most of my childhood dreams although they required hard work, determination and blessings. There are other accomplishments I wish to achieve in this life here on Earth. Therefore, I realize I must put on my walking shoes to be prepared for the long and sometimes difficult journey. When I stop dreaming, I stop living.

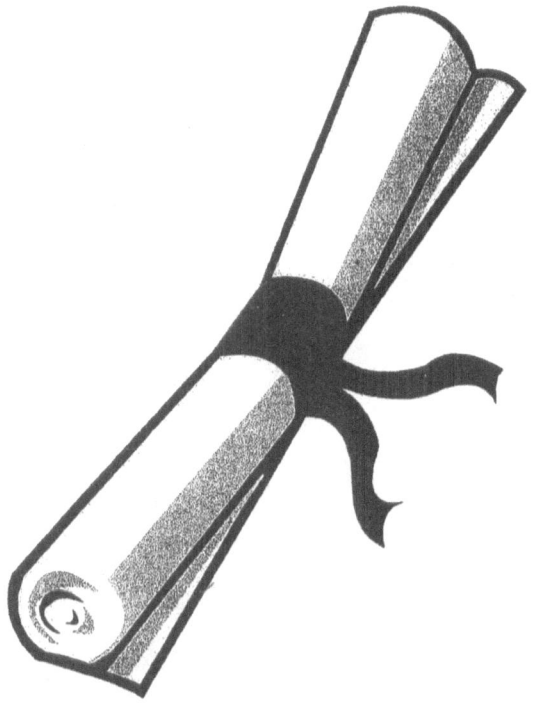

Although Low Income, there is no excuse for not getting at least a high school education. If you can not afford college you can at least be functional enough to go to trade school

My Father & Mother believed

One of my many chores were milking the cows

In today's world I am having a little trouble figuring out some of the changing trends of SOME of the younger generations. I welcome progress in the world, however some of the things I tried to move away from as a child SOME of the younger folks seem to be moving backward. Some of the things I see happening today make me scratch my head. I notice SOME of the young folk today buy expensive work boots and do not take the time to tie the boots strings nor seems to have the desire to work. Some young folks today allow their parents to buy them blue jeans that are faded, have patches on them or even holes in them when they purchase them. These were some of the things I tried to get away from. How can a person with expensive taste afford expensive things without working? If a person does not obtain a certain level of education how can they expect a descent job? I could not wait to graduate from school and get a job to get some of the many things I dreamed of as a child. Today it seems as though SOME of the young folks do not want to leave the safety of their mother and father's home and if they do they return soon after. How can a young man call himself a father if he cannot provide for his child financially or socially?

The south was famous for the saying, {shotgunwedding]. In many cases when a young lady became pregnant the parent of the young lady demanded that the young man step up to the plate, marry their daughter and face his responsibilities. In small town news quickly traveled around and it caused great embarrassment spiritually and morally if the young lady were not married. I guess that was one of the reasons for large families during that era. It was a fulltime job taking care of those large families therefore everyone had a chore to do. There was no hanging out all night and sleeping all day. As a rule while living in your parent house you had to go by the rules that they established. If you were going to school you had chores to do, if you were not going to school you had more chores to do and if you did not want to follow their demands they quickly told you to "Hit the road." For the most part there was love in the home however the kids were taught to listen and have respect. There was a time you could tell when school was out because you notice quite a few school age kids on the streets, now there seems to be a large number of school age kids on the streets whether school is in session or not.

Some of the ways I kept myself busy and out of trouble while growing up in the south were after my homework and chores were done, my buddies and I played ball and tried our luck at trying to sing. We did not have many ball diamonds, gymnasiums and modern facilities that the young folks have today. Sometimes we played in fields and at times in cow pastures. The cows normally found a shady place under a large tree. If there was not a bull in the pasture we had it made, however we had to still be a little careful because the footing could get a little nasty if we did not pick our spots carefully. Large numbers of the most skilled athletes back in the day started out with crude equipment and progress gradually to bigger and better things. Some of us could not afford baseballs and bats therefore we used tennis balls and broom sticks instead. There was a great hunger and desire to succeed in our chosen sport. That was better than standing around on the few street corners in some of the small towns. Matter of fact we were not allowed to hang around in town. Some of the older folks usually hung out in the local barber shops and share the current gossip, talked sports and often discuss the Bible. Many times they agreed and other times they had disagreements. The men usually kept the conversations clean for the most part, if women or children were present. Some of the young people today including older people as well should try to adapt a similar practice. I am not proclaiming that only southern people are good, there are good and bad all over the world. There has been huge improvement in the south since I left and young folks today have better opportunities to have a better life if they really desire, however it seems like some of the city problems have drifted south. I guess we have to take the bitter with the sweet.

In the south where I grew up everyone were not perfect. We had bootleggers, some people that were lustful, wolves in sheep clothing and false prophets, however for the most part they were good Christian people helping one another. Many of the most popular singers of yesterday and now started out in the church down south and eventually ended up singing blues, roll and roll and soul music because of the money. Later on in their careers some of them went back to gospel music where they began. Sometimes in our life we have a habit of returning to our past. Many people in the town where I grew up returned to our little town after retirement from their jobs up north or elsewhere, however my plans are to remain in Maryland. I believe a person should do what make them happy not trying to keep up with the Joneses. Sometimes we allow ourselves to be overwhelmed by life. The crushing blows of disappointments, endless debts, debilitating illness, or trouble with people can cause hopelessness, depression or despair. People seem to forget that Jesus is present with his love, compassion and grace. There was a barber in my home town who were a deacon in one of the local churches who thought he was a preacher during the week because he will quote the bible everyday to everyone that came into his shop. He would take a great amount of time to cut your hair because in between cutting your hair, turning the barber's chair, taking a half step toward the empty coffee can and spiting tobacco juice into it along with several pauses to talk about the bible you could be there half of the day. Many people do not believe in God however they get married and go through the ceremony of marriage promises to God that you will love your mate through sickness and death. The barber was married however rumors were that he had another woman on the side. As a matter of fact his wife came in one day and had a serious altercation with him and the other woman who was visiting him in the shop at that time. We must keep in mind that, {We please God when our walk matches our talk.}.

As you perhaps noticed I often mention God and Jesus throughout my life. In order to tell you about my life I must mention my Lord and savior because if it were not for his mercy and grace I would have no life to talk about. The many years of our suffering during those civil right days helped me to grow in faith. I often talked about the things I did not have, the few things that I had as well as the things I desired not realizing at the time that I had already received the greatest gift that any one could receive, {The gift of life.} If I never have a lot of money or a lot of material things, if I never become famous, I have already accomplished what I wanted to do, putting God number one in my life. According to my teaching I understand that, {God did not ask me to be famous, he only ask me to be Faithful.}

When I left my hometown in 1961 to relocate to Baltimore, one of the several advices my father emphasized to me was to make sure to join a church near me. I followed his advice however due to my work schedule I did not always attend church as often as I should. Thanks to God and his blessing I have gotten my priorities in order. Being a Disciple of Christ I now realize that no matter how busy I may be I must put God number ONE in my life.

—G.F.F.

I believe that Jesus Christ is the one foundation of the church.

Luther H. Foster High School

The name of my high school changed many years ago however it will always be Luther H. Foster to me because it bring back fond memories and was a breath of fresh air for me.

"The Mighty Bulldogs"

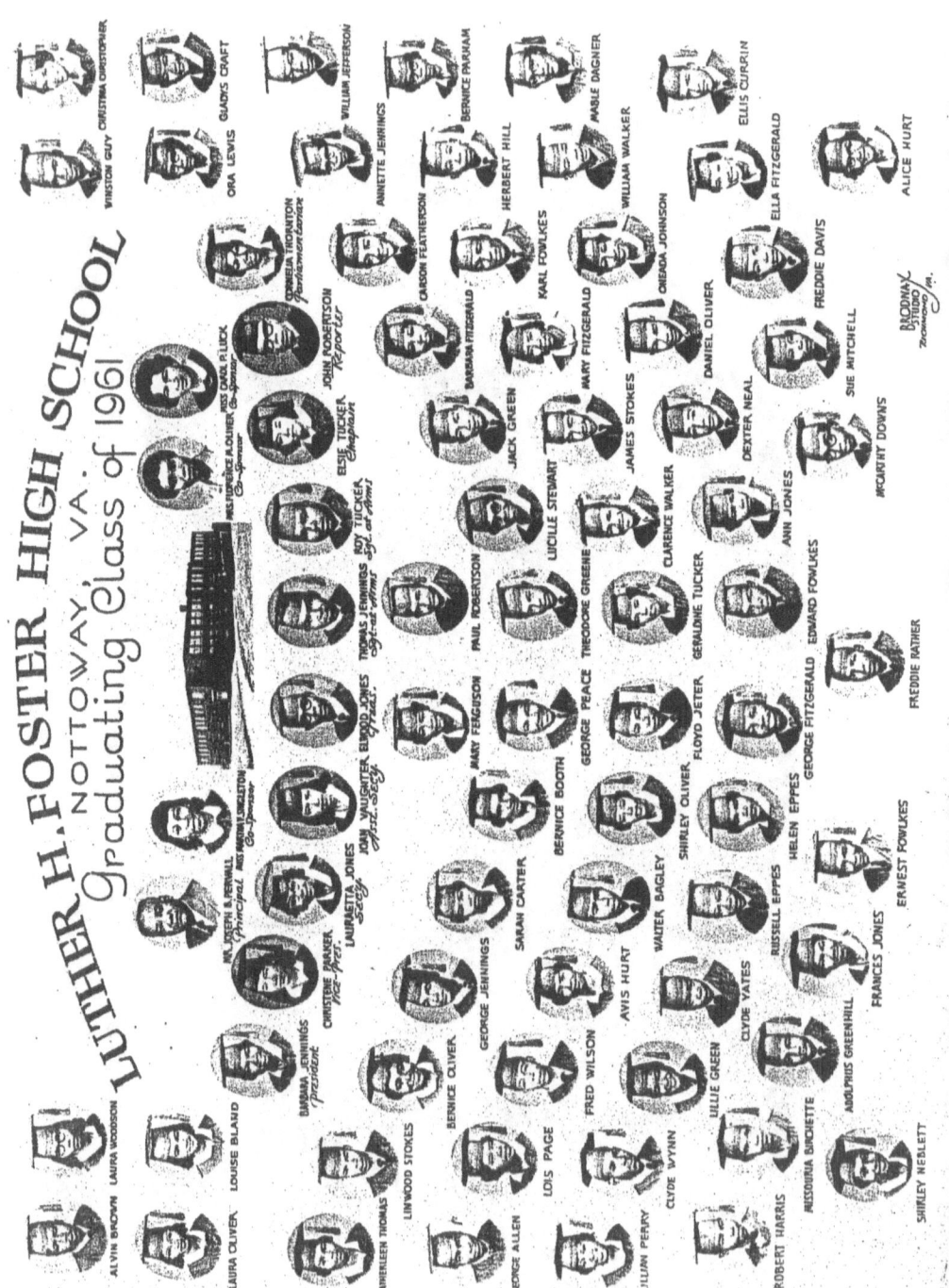

# LUTHER H. FOSTER HIGH SCHOOL
## NOTTOWAY, VA.
### Graduating Class of 1961

SHELTERS ON OUR LITTLE FARM

On our little farm we had a bam.
On our little farm we had a woodshed a few yards from our beautiful flower beds.
On our little farm we had a smoke house.
On our little farm we had a tool house.
On Our little farm we had an out house.
On our little farm we had a hen house.
On our little farm we had a dog house.
On my little farm I built myself a play house.
I do not remember if my sister ever had a doll house in the house where we lived,
But I remember my father having a shed where he kept his tractor and a little
    icebox where he kept a little bottle of joy and laugher.
I can assure you that on our little farm we did not have a pen house.

Mr. George F. Fitzgerald

The following section contains my personal beliefs about life and spirituality. It is not meant to offend anyone who may have different religious or other views, and I hope that all who read it will gain something positive from it.

# BELIEFS

## LIFE

Try to be happy and positive each and every day. Do some of the things that you desire to do without delay. "Tomorrow is not promised," as the old folks often said. As you enjoy your life, try to help someone along the way. Try to be honest and take care of your responsibilities first; if not, your situations could become worse. Be strong and stand up for righteousness. There is nothing wrong with enjoying a good Christian life. Whatever you achieve, or whatever you do, always put God first.

*The thief comes only to steal and kill and destroy; I came that they may have life, and have it abundantly.*

*John 10:10*

## CHRISTIANITY

To live a Christian life means a lot to me. Christian living demonstrates how I should live here on earth and it prepares me to deal with the hills and valleys of my existence. More importantly, good Christian living helps me to realize that I cannot serve two gods, not if I believe that God has prepared a place for me in His kingdom after my life here on earth is done. I was as glad as could be when Jesus reached out His hand to me and said, "Come follow me."

*Am I now seeking human approval, or God's approval? Or am I trying to please people? If I were still pleasing people, I would not be a servant of Christ.*

*Galatians 1:10*

## EDUCATION

Education is necessary in order to function in today's world. Do not use your education to help you to look down on people who have not reached the same level of learning that you have. Instead, try to help them, and encourage them along the way. Do not let your education go to your head, but let it continue to flow to your brain so that you can improve the lives of others. There are many people who may not have attained your level of education yet play very important roles in your life.

*Anyone who claims to know something does not yet have the necessary knowledge. But anyone who loves God is known by him.*

*1 Corinthians 8:2-3*

## MONEY AND MATERIAL THINGS

Money is essential in today's world. There are very few places that you can go without money; however, we must realize that, no matter how much we have, we cannot take it with us when we die. Jewelry, luxury cars and beautiful homes are nice to have, especially if we achieved them the honest way. We must be mindful of the fact that we did not acquire these things by ourselves. Try to help someone who is truly in need as you enjoy your successes, and thank God each and every day.

*(For every house is built by someone, but the builder of all things is God.)*

*Hebrews 3:4*

*You shall have no other gods before me.*

*Exodus 20:3*

## FRIENDS

Be careful whom you choose for a friend. True friends are not easy to find. No one can live alone; nonetheless, you must understand the difference between a friend and an associate. You can avoid many heartaches and pains if you can tell the difference. As the old folks often said, "Friends are as scarce as hen's teeth." Oh, what a friend we have in Jesus!

*. . . God is love.*

*1 John 4:8*

## MR. AND MRS. PERFECT

We should not walk around criticizing people day after day. Instead, try looking at the good in people and try looking on the bright side of life. Sometimes we must make difficult decisions, therefore, we should pray to God daily for wisdom and knowledge. If we need medical help, we should not deny it, and if we need spiritual help, we should admit it. Understand that no one is perfect. Realize that God helps those who help themselves.

*He saved us, not because of righteous things we had done, but because of his mercy . . .*

*Titus 3:5*

## POLITICIANS

Do you realized that there are someone who has more power than you, do you understand that you have someone to answer too? There can be nothing politically right if it is mortally wrong. Politicans, the rich and the famous please remember, you cannot glorify yourself and Christ at the same time. It does not matter how rich you are or how famous you may be, what happens in the dark will eventually come to the light. God give and God take away. {The best role model is Christ} Humble yourself under the mighty hand of God, that he may exalt you in due time.

Peter: 5:6

## WORK

There is a time for everything. As a young boy I were taught that one must get down on his knees and pray for what you need, then get up and go out and hustle, "THE HONEST WAY" There is no need to set around and cry, you can make it if you try.

God help those who help themselves.

---

## MEMORY

In this busy world today sometimes we seems to busy that we can not find time to slow down and smell the roses. We have gotten in the habit of taking things for granted. Some of us need to realize who created this great Heaven and earth. {Read Genesis in your Bible}

If anyone preaches any other gospel to you than what you have received, let him be accursed.

Galatians: 1:9

—

## MEMORY

Did you forget to pray today, did you bless your food today? Did you give thanks to God for allowing you to see another day? Did you ask God to put you in the right path and show you the way or do you believe you do not need him and you can do everything yourself in your own way? Freedom doesn't give us the right for self satisfaction, freedom give us the opportunity to please God. Doing God's will is the key to freedom.

The Lord is gracious and full of compassion. Psalm 111:4

Real Christians will not forget that in the good times as well in times of trouble when your enemies try to due you harm and you become confused and do not know what to do, they realized that if they put their trust in the Lord he will be their stabilizer.

You therefore must endure hardship as a good soldier of Jesus Christ.
2 Timothy 2:3

## MARRIAGE

Marriage is great if both parties really love and care for one another. Couples must spend quality time together and allow a little down time alone for each other. Trust is a must between marriage partners. Every day will not be a bed of roses; however, if your good days outnumber your bad ones, you can make it. Remember, the family that prays together usually stays together.

What God has joined together, no one can take apart.

# DRUGS

---

Some folks allow drugs to destroy their hopes and dreams some folks refuse to realize that if they really try, they can become clean. Drugs will cause a person to ignore the fact that there is a place they can go to receive help, drugs will cause a person to try to hide their addictions, not realizing that in the drug world there are no secrets kept.

Drugs will make a person seems temporary happy, however that short lived happiness will soon disappear and they find themselves all alone, drugs has caused many people to lose their happy homes.

Drugs will make a school boy forget his books, drugs will make a beauty queen forget her looks, drugs will cause one to beg, steal, and borrow, drugs will cause one to end up in a early grave causing their love ones pain and sorrow. Drugs will cause one to hurt the ones they love, and drugs will cause a person to forget that there is a God up above.

"Legal, drugs can cause the same effects if not taken properly."

STOP KILLING EACH OTHER


STAY IN SCHOOL

BABIES STOP HAVING BABIES

STOP SHOWING DISRESPECT FOR ONE ANOTHER

These are some of the ways we can help ourselves as a race of
People


SELF-HELP

Every since the existence of the world people have found a reason to discriminate, whether it is race, religion, land or social status. There are light skin black people who look down on darker skin black people, there are people who have a higher level of education that look down on people with a lesser level of learning, and there are people who have more material things including money than others who look down on the less fortunate. In the Bible, God is concerned with the well-being of widows and orphans, the poor, and the dispossessed. I am not saying that one should give their hard earn money to everyone however God want us to share a portion of our blessing with the less fortunate no matter the race, creed or color. God gave you a brain and we must use it. Solomon prayed for wisdom, so can we. If you are black and get in trouble with the law, your chances are stacked against you, however if you are white and commit the same crime or sometimes a crime that is more severe the white person stand a better chance of receiving a lesser penalty then the black person. That is not news that is something we must be aware of and try not to do so many silly things. Instead of getting involved in so many stupid acts that time should be used for helping to find ways of keeping the civil rights movement alive. We must understand that a good football team has gifted players that can throw the ball , players that can catch the ball, players that can run the ball, players that can kick the ball, players that can block and all the players need to think. After blending all their talents together in many cases hard work and a little luck spell Victory. Although we have made progress as a race the battle is not over. There is work to be done the playing field is not level.

During the early civil rights era we fought and many were injured or gave their lives in order to make things better for our future generation. With blisters on our feet we kept on moving. A large number of us went to jail in order to gain a small share of freedom. Today, too many of our young people are going to jail for stupid things. When we do so many silly things we are putting the shackles back around our ankles. Today they call it house arrest and they put an ankle bracelet around ones ankle. When I was growing up I was denied jobs or promotions because of the color of my skin. Today many employers have many reasons not to hire our people. Some of the reasons is plain to see such as too many of our young folks spend too much time hanging out in the streets instead of going to school and trying to get a level of education, instead of getting caught up in criminal activity thus building a long criminal record, not knowing how to speak or dress for a job interview, allowing themselves to be overwhelmed with laziness and a don't care attitude, allowing drugs to destroy their lives before they begin to live and much more. Young folks you should enjoy the partial freedom you have and try to build on it. I believe there is not a post civil rights movement I feel that the struggle is still going on. We should not allow ourselves to fall for that false sense of security. Young folks we need you to help carry the load as least for your children's sake. Many of you have at least one child therefore you need a job to support him or her. Today discrimination presents itself in a sneaky manner however if you pay close attention you will realize it is alive and well.

## SELF-HELP

In spite of all the cards that are stacked against us we must stop blaming others for all our problems. There are many ways we can help ourselves without waiting for an equal slice of the American dream to fall into our laps. Sometimes we are bewildered, or overwhelmed. We search for a way to make sense out of life we don't know what to do. We don't know how to begin. We yearn for a call that take us beyond ourselves generally we do not heed warnings until it too late and we hate to be told we are doing wrong. Some of us seem to lack spiritual vitality. Part of the time we deliberately rebel, we go deliberately against God. We seem to have a lack of peace within ourselves, it seems too many of us all races creed and colors are reluctant to leave the lifestyle of the secular world. As a country boy and son of a sharecropper I learned at an early age that God should be number one my life and then family. We need to examine ourselves and do a little house cleaning before it too late. The clock is ticking. The following pages will mention ways to get on the right track. I am not perfect. In Romans 3: 10 "There is no one righteous, not even one"

All you parent out there please wake up. There is a saying that goes like this "it is easier to build a child then to repair an adult." We as parent must set as example as well as teach our children at an early age right from wrong. We must take a little more time from our busy schedule to talk to our children and feel their needs. Young folks have problems and grown up have problems in life. We as parent must keep the line off communication open at all times, if we do not thugs in the street will lead your children astray. I understand sometimes it is hard with a one parent family however if you have a trusted relative or friend that might be your answer or even a trusted church member. In The Gospel According To Luke Jesus said "Let the children come to me and do not hinder them; for to such belongs the Kingdom of God." I believe our children are our future and we should raise them up to make the world a better place. We should introduce children to the church at an early age and make them aware that all people are not bad however we must teach them that all grownups are not good. We must teach them that if anyone grown up or young start acting strange they can come to you and inform you the best that that can what is happening. In many cases the social workers do not realize what is happening to some of our innocent children. This nonsense happens every day and it is not restricted to any special race or relations. Sometimes it is necessary to build a wall of protection around your child because there can be verbal abuse as well as physical abuse. I feel every good parent would like for their children to grow up and be the best that they can be, however you must invest time in your children. If you truly take the time to teach them when they are young the employer will have fewer reasons not to hire them or deny them when they enter the job market.

Young folks as well as older folks we must learn to get along among one another, we must grow up and help make this world a better place. We need to control our anger and use that energy for something positive. We must learn that everyone do not have the same opinion. We need to have respect for one another and control our anger. We must learn that it's ok to agree to disagree and move on within harming anyone. People are coming to America from all over the globe. It is very essential that we as a race establish a place for us in this society instead of spending most of our lives in jail. We should not harm or kill anyone but we continue to rape, rob and kill our own people. If anyone desires to kill or harm someone why not join the army and help defend some of the freedoms we have before we give it all back. There is no freedom in jail. Most newcomers that came to America had a hard time at first because it was not easy to start a new life in an unfamiliar country. Most immigrants had to learn a new language and a new way of life. Look around you and see who own most everything. We must not give back the little freedoms that our parent, grand-parent and great grand-parent fought and died for. New immigrants made their lives a little better by finding friends from their native country and lived together in small neighborhoods. We must learn to live together without killing one another.

## PARENTIAL GUIDANCE

Researches, scientist and health officials cannot teach our children how to live each day. We as parents must set the example, we must show our children the way. Health officials can only inform us of what is good and what is bad. At an early age children must learn from their moms and their dads. We must teach our children how to read the difference warning labels and help them understand that according to clinical studies smoking and many other substances can be very harmful to their health. Let them know that addiction to many substances affects the poor and also those who possesses wealth. Keep the line of communication open between you and your children; teach. them to be strong, teach them the difference between right and wrong. Unhealthy lifestyle is not only bad for the young; it is bad for everyone.

## CHOICES

My father was a sharecropper who grew all kinds of crops including tobacco. The black folks in the community called him Mr. Albert. I hated tobacco from day one because it required a lot of work. I was afraid to raise my voice, because I had no choice. If I had my way I would rather grow fruits, vegetables and pretty flowers that could be pollinated by the birds and the bees. I would rather grow beautiful trees and things that we need. As I grew older I realized my father had to do what he had to do. Many things he taught has came true. My father had passed on, God bless his soul. I will meet him in heaven one day, that's what I believe, that's what I believe, that's what I been told.

## FOODFUL THOUGHTS

If you are willing, if you are able please push that chair away from the dinner table. If you sneak to eat and do not get caught eventfully everyone will know and it will be your fault. It's not easy. We understand, however if you do not try you are to blame. If you keep it off you will not have to take it off. Your quality life is at stake, it may depend on the choices you make. I know it's hard, but you cannot give in, today is the day you must start.

## VERY DANGEROUS

Do I smell smoke, have you lost your mind, have your lost your head? Oh no I hope you are not smoking in bed. Smoking in bed is very dangerous, it could cause a fire, that addictive habit could result in our love ones and neighbors finding US all dead. Bad habits are hard to break, for pete sake', help is out there for you. If you cannot break the habit on your own, if you find yourself in that position seek help, you need to talk to your physician.

## WHAT'S IN IT FOR ME?

There's tar in cigarettes that sticks to the lining of your lungs eventually making it difficult to breathe . We need to breathe all day and all night, shortness of breath is something you do not need . . . There are chemicals in cigarettes including carbon monoxide that could poison your lungs. To make the right decision you must not give in, you must be strong. If you are smart, if you are bright, say no and help keep your smile beautiful and your teeth white.

## TRY AGAIN

If you attempt to quit smoking or any bad lifestyle habits, don't give up, do not quit. The fact that you gave in the first time that not the end of it. That do not mean you cannot win. Many people fail the first time and they do not give up, they try again. Don't be a coward, be brave and put your best foot forward. Tell yourself, courage is something that you do not lack, pick yourself up and get back on track. Don't be ashamed to ask for support, it's no harm to admit you can not do it alone. The life you save may be your own.

## THAT'S A NONO

You cannot smoke in this car because I do not enjoy the smell of cigarettes. You cannot smoke in this car because I fear for my health being around second hand smoke from your cigarette knowing what they contains nicotine, carbon monoxide and tar. . You cannot smoke in this building you have to go outside, can't you see the signs, can't you see the tears coming from: my eyes? Don't be silly this is a non-smoking facility. You cannot smoke in this house, not only are you putting your health at risk? You could be harming my pets including my bird cat and dog. You could cause damage to my furniture my carpet and my rug. I apologize you have to take that cigarette out side

## SHOW LOVE FOR YOUR CHILD

Future dad, do you realize while smoking you may be damaging your sperm that could cause difficulties in fertilization? Please beware, please protect God's creation. Babies produced from damaged sperm could have an increased risk of childhood health problem including acute leukemia, lymphoma and cancers. If you have not started smoking or if you have started smoking, please STOP, that could be the answer. You need to stop before it's too late, because a woman's partner that smokes near her during her pregnancy could raise the risk of delivering a baby that weights too little and have serious health concerns. It better to stop now instead or saying I am sorry it is a lesson learned.

## ALL THAT GLITTERS IS NOT GOLD

Do not be attracted by tobacco companies' advertisement, in the end with health problems that cigarettes could cause may end in great disappointment. Most health officials and researchers believe that smoking is not a wise thing to do. Smoking is not something your body needs, smoking is not something you must do. If your friends smoke that do not mean that you must do it too. Young people, smoking does not make you an adult, smoking does not make you a woman or a man. Your refusal to smoke could save you lots of money and more importantly-lots of heartaches and pain. Part of being an adult means making wise decisions and smart choices. If you truly love someone who smokes ask them to stop, seek help if necessary. Don't be afraid to lift up your voice.

## FUTURE ATHLETE?

Mr. Mrs. or Miss Athlete, how do think you will be able to compete if you are weak. If you have little stamina and unable to breathe in the heat of the battle-you will simply fall to your knees. Talk to your health officials, talk to your coach. Discuss with them the goals you are .trying to reach and the achievements you will like to approach. Those dreams requires a healthy lifestyle and healthy lungs, you must be strong. Most health official and researches believe smoking increase the chance of causing damage to your respiratory system and lungs. If your dreams are to become an athlete please try to understand my grammar, you need stamina.

## PLEASE BE STRONG

Hey young lady, hey young man, if you have not started smoking please do not start. If you have already started you should stop if you consider yourself smart. Studies have proven smoking could be a serious health risk. Do you want to be added to an early fatality list? Take care of your heart and lungs. Leave the leaves in the fields and the added ingredients in the laboratories where they belong. According to many health officials, to smoke is not a joke.

## READ THE LABELS

Are you aware how smoking cigarettes can affect you? Have you taken the time to read the labels, do you have a clue? The deadly gas called carbon monoxide do not belong inside of your lungs. Some smoke for peer pressure, some smoke thinking it reduces stress and some smoke thinking it cool. Don't be a fool, in the end in many cases the smoker is the one who lose.

## "ATTENTION"

Take that cigarette out of your mouth, put that cigarette out. Take that pack of cigarettes out of your pocket and throw them away. Say what you may, you need to stop without further delay. Your lungs will thank you and your heart will thank you to. Although to quit smoking may be a huge challenge, remember quality life may be in the balance. It's not easy to rid yourself of the craving for nicotine however it's a huge challenge you must overcome to have a better chance of fulfilling your dreams.

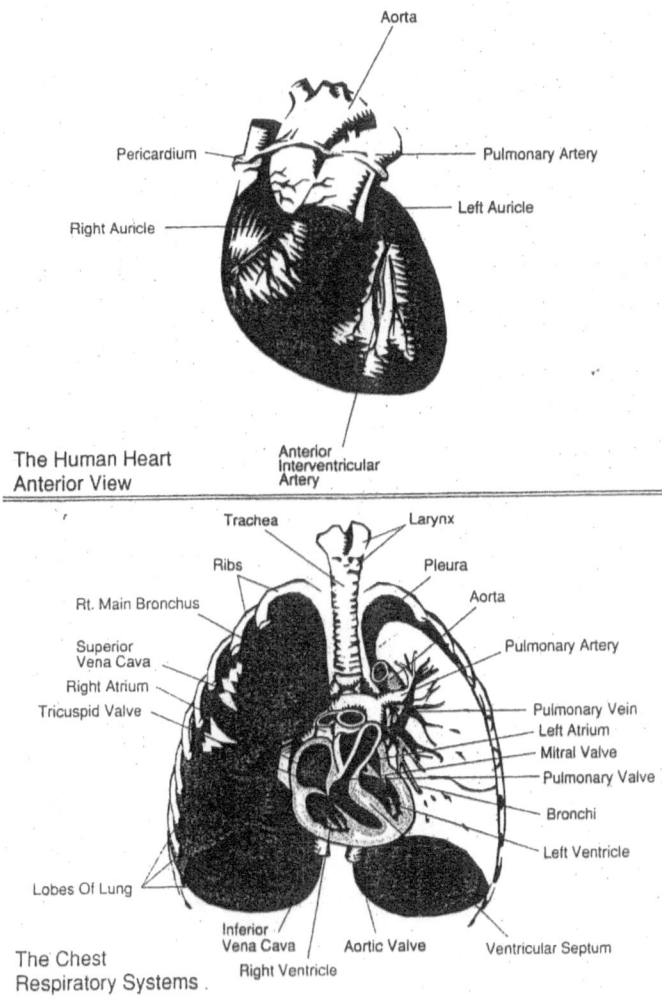

The Human Heart
Anterior View

The Chest
Respiratory Systems

## INCREASING YOUR CHANCE FOR LONGEVITY

Things that you must do for your body in order for it to function in an efficient manner, must be done in moderation. Things that your body have no need for that will harm your body, once your are aware of it, you should not start or if you have already started you should quit. In order for you to feel at your peak, you need to reduce stress and get proper sleep. Exercise and a proper diet are essential to help keep your body in tip top condition. Remember that a long and healthy life is your mission. It is very important that you confer with your doctor and health officials.

## A WEIGHTY PROBLEM

Smoking is not a way to escape, smoking is not a healthy way of losing weight Exercise and a healthy diet is the key. Its good for you and good for me. Think about it, dragging on a cigarette is not the answer, especially If you Increase your chance of lung cancer. Please acknowledge to quit smoking sometimes it takes will power and sometimes it takes knowledge. Don't be afraid to seek support from positive associates and if needed help from health officials.

## COCAINE

Cocaine is a drug made from the leaves of the coca plant. The coca plant is a evergreen shrub with reddish bark and yellowish-green flowers . . . . Cocaine affects the young the famous and fathers and mothers. It sometimes brings the worst in people, sometimes causing them to become violent and out of control. The trouble that cocaine causes often takes a heavy toll. Cocaine can also create a disturbance in the brain's electrical signals, that drug can cause a person and people around them lots of pain. Cocaine can cause death, cocaine can drive a person insane. Some sources said doctors once used cocaine to treat pain such as toothache and ear aches. Cocaine also stimulates an area in the brain that regulates pleasurable sensations. Cocaine is the cause of many of drug related crimes all over the nation. Dilated pupils is another sign of someone using cocaine, oh what a shame. Cocaine comes in different forms and are all addictive.

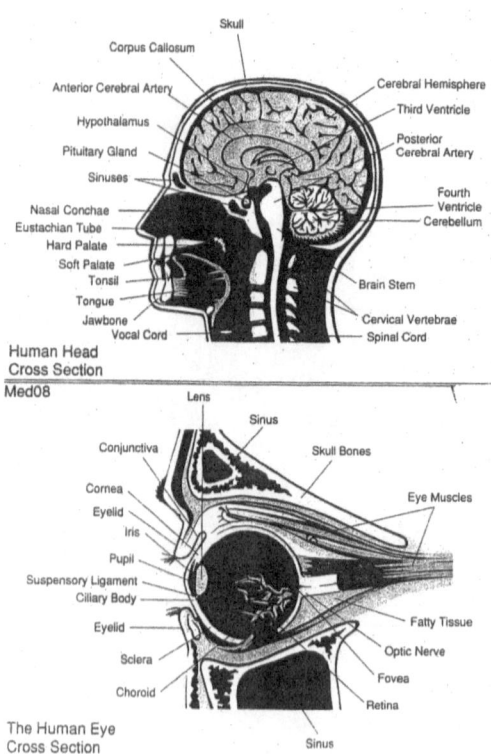

## THE MORNING AFTER

It was still dark as I stumbled out of bed heading for the bath room . with my stomach rumbling and pains streaking through my aching head. It was the day after new years. I said to myself, that's the price I must pay for consuming all those cheers. I thought to myself I have not felt this bad since last year, I sure had a good time maybe when my head and stomach mend I may decide to do it next year all over again.

## RELEASE THE BOTTLE

After drinking a bottle of booze and nearly a keg of beer. your monstrous voice is all I hear. You been here you been there If one believe you they'll think you been everywhere. You make promises you cannot keep. You irritate the strong as well as the meek As soon as you get home you are ready to eat and quickly go fast asleep. Please make up your mind to put that bottle down . Then you will stop acting like a clown Seek the Lord , Whatever troubling you than and only than at the river side you can lay your burdens down.

## A DRUNKEN MOMENT

For one drunken moment you struck me and cursed me and you also wished I were dead and in hell. The very next day you asked me to forgive you and asked me not to tell. Some of the words you used were more that I could bear. Although I love you there will be no next time. Today I am drawing the line. If you only took the time to listen to yourself while enjoying your bottle maybe you would be ashamed. I am through playing this dangerous game. Maybe after I am gone you will wake up and understand.

## IF YOU TRULY LOVE YOUR CHILD

Do not allow your baby to involuntary become a passive smoker. The nicotine and other irritants in tobacco smoke passes into the placenta that carries blood and nutrients from the mother's body directly into the baby's body. This could cause the baby not to be healthy strong and hardy. Smoking could cause an increase in miscarriages and low birth Weight, please stop before it's too late.

## THINK TWICE

Please do not sniff that glue, can't you think of anything better to do? Sniffing certain inhalant can cause serious damaged to your brain. Your brain suppose to be the organ of thought and nervous coordination. Don't give in to peer pressures, yield not to temptation.

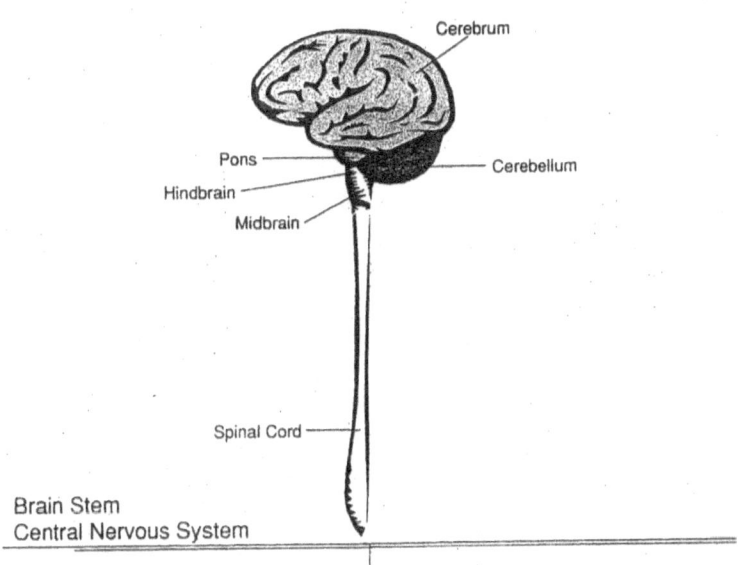

Brain Stem
Central Nervous System

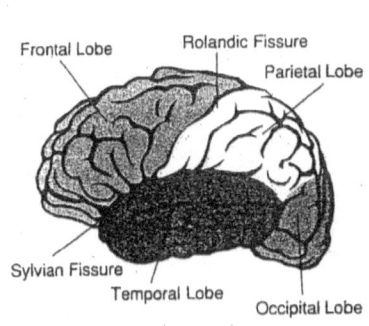

Human Brain
Brain - Lateral View

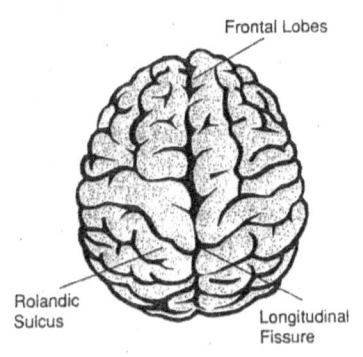

Human Brain
Cerebral Hemispheres

## YOU MUST PAY A PRICE

You are wrong if you think you can. take a magic pill or injection to make you big and strong. At the time it may seem nice, but in the end you will certainly pay a price. Great athletic achievements comes as a result of natural abilities, healthy diets, discipline, training and dedication. If you put your heart mind and soul into what you truly want to achieve there will be no need for cheating to reach your goals.

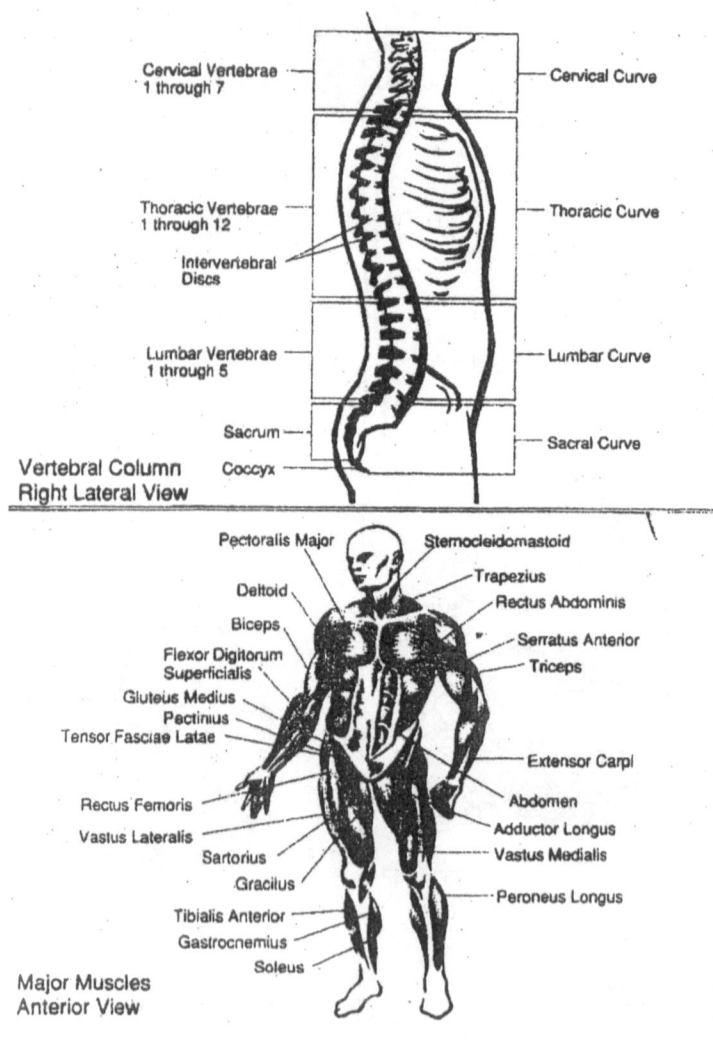

## THE ALMIGHTY DOLLAR

You run around every day and half of the night chasing that almighty dollar. As you allows money to consume your soul and your mind there will be times when things go wrong and you will be the first to holler. Remember you came into this world naked. At times in your life you wondered how you were going to make it. You are forgetting a very important lesson. You fail to realize from whom cometh all blessing. When all is said and done you will find out that money is not number one.

## ROLLING THE DICE

The rolling of the dice could greatly affect you and your family's life. Things that you and your family essentially needs may be sacrificed. Gambling can become an addiction, if someone tells you different it's not true, it's simply fiction. In most cases you will not reap the rewards you have projected. Meanwhile you and your family could be neglected. I hate to be the messenger of bad news but could the owners of those establishments be saying heads I win and tales you lose?

## TALENTS HOPES AND DREAMS

Put away that knife every puncture could let out the air of someone's hopes and dreams. You must allow everyone to live out their hopes and dreams. Inside of man there are many talents and positive things for mankind to accomplish some of which you have not yet seen. Don't sell that child dope we cannot afford to let that child talent hopes and dreams go up in smoke. Put that gun away. God give many talents you have a talent you can Display. Put away that broom do not try to sweep that young girl off of her feet A child should not have a child. That young lady has her education to complete. It's a shame people like you have caused so much pain and many talents hopes and dreams to go down the drain.

## TRY JESUS

Have you been trying and trying to overcome your addictions are you so confused and weary you don't know which way to turn? Let me tell you about a lesson I have learned. Are you ready to give up, wipe those tears from your eyes, don't cry, give Jesus a try. If you have tried everything including doctors, hypnosis or even acupuncture and failed, try Jesus because he will always prevail. Believe in the Lord, trust in the Lord and ask him to help you, he will surely see you through.

## DISCLAIMER

I am not a doctor, scientist or a health official, however after reading and talking to various health officials my strong opinion is that the use of tobacco products and other addictive substances as well as worshiping material things can be very hazardous to your health and well-being

## PLEASE SEEK ADVICE FROM YOUR DOCTOR OR OTHER HEALTH OFFICIALS

## ROSA

Sir let me make it clear let me repeat, I am not giving up my seat. I am tired there is no doubt do you realize that some of us on this bus have just finished scrubbing and cleaning your mama's house? I am tired from my head to my feet I am not giving up my seat. I paid my fare and I am a human being just like you, go on do what you have to do. As you become older some of you white folks heart seems to become colder I am a human being just like you so go on do what you have to do I am not trying to be tough you must understand enough is enough. I am not going to allow you to walk all over me. No I am not giving up my seat. I have been cleaning and sewing all day long, tell me what have I done wrong? No I am not giving up my seat until my journey is complete. This stand is not just for me because when all our people band together we shall be free.

www.ingramcontent.com/pod-product-compliance
Lightning Source LLC
Chambersburg PA
CBHW031255280526
45784CB00004B/1861